Fasting, Prayer and Tithing

Fasting, Prayer and Tithing
The Renewal and Transformation of Worship

Cherry Brown-Graham

ISBN: 978-976-97204-0-4

Edited by: Karlene Murray (KarTaMur Professional Services)

The Scripture quotations are taken from the King James Version Bible. (2012). Zondervan

DEDICATION

To my late husband, Patrick Anthony "Bunny" Graham, whose unwavering love, confidence, support, and belief in my abilities remain with me and continue to motivate me in my writing endeavours.

CONTENTS

Acknowledgements i

Introduction 1

1 What is Fasting, Prayer & Tithing? 3

2 Worship Is Essential, But What Is Worship? 5

3 Fasting 8

4 Fasting In Action 10

5 Prayer 12

6 Results of Prayer 16

7 Tithing 18

8 Benefits of Tithing 21

9 Conclusion 23

10 Personal Evaluation 26

Bibliography 28

About The Author 29

ACKNOWLEDGEMENTS

I acknowledge with deepest gratitude the assistance received from various individuals in completing this publication.

First, I must thank Almighty God for His enduring grace that has sustained me from conception to completion of this book.

I want to express special thanks to the late Pansy M. Porteous, Supervisor extraordinaire, who guided me from the topic selection to the final draft of a study from which this book was birthed. She was truly a paragon of endurance, patience, and perseverance. She went beyond the call of duty.

I give special thanks to Rev. Hyacinth Edwards, the Board of Elders, and Members of the Salem United Church for their support.

It would be remiss to conclude without thanking my family for offering moral support and helping me successfully complete the original project. A special thank you to Phylicia and Carima, my daughters, who helped me type and accompanied me into the wee hours of the morning while I worked. You have all been a source of inspiration.

INTRODUCTION

The power of the Church has long been accepted, at least in the Western Hemisphere. Youngblood (1995) defines the Church as a local assembly of believers as well as the redeemed of all ages who follow Jesus Christ as Saviour and Lord.

From the formation of the early Christian Church, the institution was mandated to be the standard bearer for truth, values, and integrity as dictated in the scriptures. **Philippians 4:8** states categorically that children of God should concentrate on; ***"whatsoever things are true, whatsoever things are honest, whatsoever things are just, whatsoever things are pure, whatsoever things are of good report; if there be any virtue, and if there be any praise, think on these things."***

Jamaica, a country of 10,991 square kilometres, is recorded in the Guinness Book of World Records as having the most churches per square kilometre in the world. The majority of Jamaicans claim to be Christians. Whether or not this is so, a certain amount of reverence is accorded to the church. When calamities arise, the first outcry usually is, "What is the Church doing?" The Church needs to pray. When things go wrong, the Preacher requests that members stretch their hands out to those who are vulnerable.

Smith (1991) states that the function of the church is to minister to human needs and worship God, Who is worthy to be praised. The writer sees worship as an integral part of the Christian existence. This worship, he states, presupposes our acceptance of the fact that God is man's sovereign Lord. When we worship, we acknowledge our dependence on Him and give Him gratitude for His goodness to mankind. There are principles in the Bible that the Church is expected to use as guidelines for Christian living. These are love, joy, peace, longsuffering, gentleness, goodness, faith, meekness, and temperance.

1st Corinthians 13 reminds believers that we are like sounding brass or a tinkling cymbal without charity. In addition to being charitable the Christian is expected to adhere to certain Biblical principles in order to experience spiritual growth.

Different churches observe the Biblical principles in different ways. There are churches where fasting services are practically mandatory. In contrast, in others, the decision to fast is totally up to the believer. As it relates to tithing, there are churches in which tithing is done by salary deduction, while in others, the regularity and amount are entirely up to the giver. The observance of Biblical principles of tithing, prayer, and fasting has produced miraculous results since the Old Testament days. Abraham gave of his increase, and the Lord made him the Father of Nations; Daniel prayed and was untouched by lions when thrown into their den; and Jesus Himself fasted at decisive moments in His life.

I believe the modern-day church can experience similar miraculous results if the believers return to living the way the Bible teaches.

CHAPTER 1

WHAT IS FASTING, PRAYER & TITHING?

FASTING

Merzer et al. (1993) define fasting as the abstinence from all food to show a dependence on God and a submission to His will. They further state that the great Jewish national and liturgical fast was that of the Day of Atonement (Leviticus 16: 29 – 34). However, fasting was generally recognized, especially after the exile as a meritorious, pious practice and a potent aid to prayer.

It is the experience of Fletcher (1995) that fasting removes the barriers to communication with God and allows the spirit man to commune directly with the heavenly Father- without disturbance. Based on these definitions, I deduce that fasting as a form of worship by church members is needed in order to slay self and worship God in spirit and truth.

PRAYER

Hayford (2000) defines prayer as invading the impossible, as the united assembly of believers expresses worship in praise and thanksgiving. The hymn writer John Wesley states that

God will do nothing on earth except in answer to believing prayer. Coogan (1993) believes that prayer is not just asking God for something; it is standing on God's side to declare that man wants what God wants.

I am aware of the power of prayer and believe that any worship experience can be enhanced if individuals dedicate themselves to prayer.

TITHING

Bernard (2010) defines tithing as an act by which we acknowledge that God is both our Sovereign Lord and the source of everything we possess. The writer refers to St. Luke 11:42, where, as recorded throughout Christian history, tithing has been taught as an ideal of Christian giving, which is the believer's normal act of gratitude to God.

According to Ridolfo (2005), from ancient times, the tenth part of a person's income or property has been devoted to religious use as an offering that demonstrates that we have put God first in our lives. Tithing is also referred to as an investment in God. This can be seen in **Malachi 3:10**, where worshippers are admonished to; ***"Bring ye all the tithes into the storehouse, that there may be meat in my house... that there shall not be room enough to receive it."***

I am convinced that tithing is a Biblical principle that will enhance the worship experience and significantly benefit every believer.

CHAPTER 2

WORSHIP IS ESSENTIAL, BUT WHAT IS WORSHIP?

According to Gill (2000), "Worship is to quicken the conscience by the holiness of God, to purge the imagination by the beauty of God, to open the heart to the love of God, and to devote the will to the purpose of God."

Worship is one of the principles of Christianity regarded as essential to an understanding of the relationship that should exist between God and man. Unger (1995) defines worship as the act of paying divine honour to a deity, religious reverence, and deference. The Hebrew word for worship is shachah, which means to bow down and prostrate oneself before another in order to give God honour and reverence. Von Allmen (2000) describes worship as the epiphany of the church because it sums up the history of salvation, which enables the church to become conscious of itself and to confess that it belongs to God.

An explanation of the term worship is given by McArthur (1995). He states that the word worship comes from the Anglo-Saxon source of the English word, which means

'Worthscripe,' which relates to the concept of worthiness. This, therefore, suggests that worship is ascribing to God His stature and affirming His supreme value. The writer expands the definition by pointing out that the Greek word for worship is 'Proskuneo,' which means to kiss the hands towards another in reverence, to kneel or prostrate to do homage.

According to biblical teachings on worship, true worship requires devotion of the whole heart, soul, mind, and strength, (St. Luke 10:27). It also requires worshipping God in Spirit and in Truth as recorded in St. John 4:24, which states that; "God is a Spirit: and they that worship Him must worship Him in spirit and in truth" and worshipping in humility for God is Holy. (Psalm 99).

According to Youngblood (1995), worship is reverent devotion and allegiance pledged to God; it is the rituals or ceremonies by which this reverence is expressed. Worship, which comes from the English word 'worthship', denotes the worthiness of the one receiving special honour or devotion.

Omartian (2004) states that worship is fulfilling the purpose of praising God. It is fulfilling a duty and setting aside time for what God expects of us. The writer adds that worship opens a door behind an individual who will find the purpose and destiny for his/her life. This definition of worship seems to be the one most practiced in our churches today. The theme of praise in worship is promoted in all religious denominations. I wish to state, however, that worship can be empty and lacking in spirituality if it is not done with a single purpose.

Chambers (2004) believes worship is giving God the best that He has given you. He believes that we should give back to God what He has given to us as a love gift in the form of worship. He believes that we should take time to meditate before God and offer the blessing back to Him in deliberate acts of worship.

Collins (1988) reminds the church that the purpose of worship is to quicken the conscience by the holiness of God, to feed the mind with the truth of God, to purge the imagination with the beauty of God, to open the heart to the love of God and to devote the will to the purpose of God. In the same light, the Westminster Catechism states that worship is the chief end and the duty of man, which is to glorify God and enjoy Him forever.

In agreeing with the above opinion, Hayford and Hammond (2004) state that worship transcends our weakness while acknowledging God's power. Worship is the secret place that hides the heart from the advances of the enemy. From this perspective, worship quickens the conscience through God's holiness, purges the imagination by the beauty of God, opens the heart to the love of God, and devotes the will to the purpose of God.

According to White (2005), Christian worship is characterized by the worshipper's conception of God and his relationship with God. The writer posits that nothing glorifies God more than a human being made holy through the worship experience. She further asserts that Christian worship is God's revelation of Himself in Jesus Christ and man's response. It is also her belief that worship is a reciprocal relationship; God takes the initiative in addressing us through Jesus Christ, and we respond with a variety of emotions and words. The writer adds that genuine worship frees us from the bondage of preconceived notions and fake religion.

Smith (1991) postulates that worship is an integral part of Christian existence and presupposes one's acceptance of the fact of God's creatorship and sovereignty. To worship is to acknowledge one's dependence upon God and, therefore, one's indebtedness to God. He argues that our worship of the living God is not meant to be dull, cold, starchy, and an immaculately orderly performance; rather, it is a passion that burns in the heart of Jesus.

This passion is not, however, uncontrolled emotionalism, as some worshippers and denominations demonstrate, but a burning heart that glorifies God and is cognizant of the mandate given to worshippers, which is to love our neighbours as ourselves.

CHAPTER 3

FASTING

Fasting is one of the Biblical principles that many people know about but scarcely adhere to. In some churches, some members fast occasionally, but this principle is not set aside as one of the requirements of their Christian stewardship.

Metzer et al. (1993) define fasting as the abstinence from all food to show dependence on God and submission to His will. After the Exodus from Egypt, the children of Israel were admonished to fast. In Leviticus 16: 29 – 34, we are told that in time, the great national liturgical fast was that of the Day of Atonement, but fasting was generally recognized, especially after the exile, as a meritorious pious practice and as a potent aid to prayer.

According to Youngblood (2000), fasting is voluntarily going without food or drink, generally for religious purposes. Jesus insisted that fasting was unnecessary for His disciples as long as He, the Bridegroom, was with them (St. Matthew 9: 14 – 15; St. Mark 2: 18 – 20; St. Luke 5: 33 – 35).

The writer points out that fasting was an important duty undertaken by the majority of Christians in the early days of the Church. Then, Godly men of the Old Testament, such as Elijah, Ezra, and Daniel, all fasted. He also observes that not only men of the Old Testament fasted but also Jesus, Cornelius, Paul, and other early church leaders fasted. I firmly believe that if fasting were not important and biblical, Jesus would never have fasted.

According to Ridolfi (2005), fasting for Christians is essential because it means they are determined to walk from victory to victory. He says that fasting builds up faith to accomplish the victory walk. He adds that fasting removes the weaknesses in the Christian's life and leaves those who fast strong to face life's battles.

He further asserts that fasting destroys pride, something that we all struggle with at regular intervals in our lives. Fasting produces humility of one's spirit. It makes individuals teachable. He argues that fasting will never take down a believer. Instead, when the church as a body develops the regular habit of fasting, it can only go upward spiritually.

Rodgers (2006) firmly believes that fasting can end the demonic attack on families and generational curses. He states that whenever individuals fast, they lay a new foundation. He further posits that there are wrong reasons to fast. According to him, people do not fast to gain merit with God or to get rid of sin. He further states that only one thing gives us merit with God and cleanses us from sin – the blood of Jesus Christ. However, fasting will bring to the surface areas of compromise in an individual's life and make one more aware of any sin in one's life so that one can repent.

According to McGuckin (2004), besides spiritual growth, there is no better way for followers of Christ to improve their health and receive divine healing than by fasting. This is because fasting and prayer enable individuals to conquer the flesh and selfish desires of the age and provide strength to walk in the Spirit of God. Prayer and fasting make us sensitive to hearing the voice of God so that we can gain the direction we need for our lives. Fasting brings revival and transformation.

CHAPTER 4

FASTING IN ACTION

The attributes of fasting were confirmed in a message by one church leader recently in my local congregation. She testified of the positive effects of fasting. She stated that the roof of their church had gone bad and needed repairs. The members of the church, situated in a remote rural area, were faced with financial challenges as the majority of the members were either unemployed or self-employed. She said they realized they needed a miracle from God, so the members decided to go on a one-week fast. She said that at the end of the week, a group of missionaries visited the area and, seeing the church's plight, re-roofed the building in a week. That preacher stated categorically that fasting is a requirement of God's people because it is through fasting that we acknowledge our total dependence on Him.

Hayford (2000) argues, however, that fasting must not be seen as a tool to twist the arm of God so that He can give us exactly what we want. Fasting has a spiritual purpose: to get our flesh out of the way so that the Spirit of God can move in our lives. Fasting helps sharpen our expectancy, so we expect to receive when we ask. Fasting removes the barriers to communication with God. It allows the spirit man to commune directly with the heavenly Father- without disturbance or interference.

Fletcher (1995) believes that the 20th century church has become so powerless because it has lost the Godly biblical customs of prayer and fasting and has succumbed to the sin of gluttony and selfishness. The writer points out that certain strongholds in our lives can only be broken down by prayer and fasting.

It is recorded in the Gospels that Jesus accepted fasting as a natural discipline. We are told in St. Matthew 4:2 that Jesus deliberately fasted before He started His ministry. Jesus' disciples, however, according to Metzer (1993), appeared not to have fasted as they were in the presence of the 'Bridegroom,' thus making fasting inappropriate and unnecessary at the time. Jesus Himself, when questioned by His disciples about their inability to heal a lunatic boy that was brought to them, told them that the power to heal requires a certain infilling as stated in St. Matthew 17:21 – that power has a three-fold force – prayer, fasting, and giving.

CHAPTER 5

PRAYER

According to John Wesley, God will do nothing on earth except in answer to believing prayer.

Youngblood (1995), in his extensive teachings on prayer, states that prayer is communication with God. He says devout good works cannot replace prayer in a needy world. Effective prayer must be a scriptural response by persons saved by grace to the living God, who can hear, and answer based on Christ's payment of the penalty that sinners deserve. The writer states that prayer involves several essential aspects. These include worship, confession, adoration, praise, thanksgiving, dedicated action, request, and effectiveness. In worship, we recognize what is of the highest worth- not ourselves, others, or our work, but God. Only the highest divine being deserves our highest respect. Guided by scripture, we set our values according to God's perfect standards.

Hayford (2000) argues that prayer is not only a response to God's grace that has been brought to us in the life and work of Jesus and the teaching of Scripture; it is also a request for our needs and the needs of others. Prayer is a request to a personal Lord who answers as He knows best. The writer expands the discourse by stating that prayer meets inner needs. One who prays will receive freedom from fear (Psalm 118: 5 -6); strength of soul (Psalm 138: 3); guidance and satisfaction (Isaiah 5: 9 – 11); wisdom and understanding (Daniel 9: 20 – 27); deliverance from harm (Joel 2:32); reward (St. Matthew 6:6); good gifts (St. Luke 11:13); fulness of joy (St. John 16: 24); peace (Philippians 4: 6 – 8) and freedom from anxiety (1st Peter 5: 7).

McGuckin (2004) states that two types of prayer are known in the teachings and examples of the New Testament Church. There is private prayer when we think of the instructions of the Sermon on the Mount (**St. Matthew 6: 5 – 8**): *"And when thou prayest…. Be not ye therefore like unto them: for your Father knoweth what things ye have need of, before ye ask Him."* Private prayers also seem to be effective. In **St. Luke 11:13**, Jesus said unto them, *"…If ye then, being evil, know how to give good gifts unto your children: how much more shall your heavenly Father give the Holy Spirit to them that ask Him?"*

Jesus recommended that believers live prayerful lives. This command is supported in St. Luke 18: 1 – 14. Jesus taught His disciples the corporate prayer.

There are also "private" prayers of Jesus Himself. He prayed at the critical moments of His life as shown in St. Luke – at His baptism (3:21) *"…that Jesus also being baptized and praying, the heaven opened"*, at the choosing of the twelve (6:12-13) *"And it came to pass in those days, that he went out into a mountain to pray, and continued all night in prayer to God. And when it was day, he called unto him his disciples: and of them he chose twelve;"*, at His transfiguration (9:28) and at His agony in the garden (22: 39-45; Hebrews 5:7). Jesus prayed.

There is no doubt that Jesus- as He lived – prayed **(St. Luke 23:46)** *"And when Jesus had cried with a loud voice, He said, Father, into Thy hand I commend my spirit: and* *having said that He gave up the ghost."* Jesus prayed even at the point of death.

Omartian (2004), in her discourse, says that prayer is not just asking God for something. For the church to pray means that it stands on God's side to declare that man wants what God wants. The writer explains that the church's prayer ministry is a prayer on earth that results in a move in heaven. The prayer of the church means that God wants to do something. The church prays about that matter first so that it can be fulfilled, and God's goal can be accomplished. In agreeing with Omartian, I concur that prayer is not a piece of antique religious furniture to be displayed on special occasions like an ornament; it is instead a way of life on the Christian journey.

The New Testament highlights many texts focusing on prayer including those of Jesus and Paul. Jesus not only taught His disciples about prayer; He gave them words to pray. In **St. Matthew 6: 5-13**, in teaching His disciples to pray, Jesus told them, *"And when thou prayest, thou shalt not be as the hypocrites are.....but when ye pray......After this manner therefore pray ye: our Father which art in heaven, Hallowed be thy Name...For thine is the kingdom, and the power, and the glory, forever, Amen."* Jesus Himself is portrayed as praying at each decisive moment in His life. Jesus is known to have prayed an entire night, as recorded in St. Luke 6:12. His prayers in St. Luke 9:29 were so intense that His very features were altered. Like Jesus, we need to know when to go to our prayer mountain to ask God to remove temptation from us and for His will to be done in our lives, as recorded in St. Luke 22: 39 – 46. St John 15:17 also outlines decisive moments in Jesus' life when He relied on the power of prayer.

Distinctively, Christians are reminded that prayer, though directed to God (Romans 1:8; 1st Corinthians 1:4; Colossians 1:3), is to be "through Jesus Christ (Romans 1:8) or in the Name of Jesus (St. John 15:17). He spoke also of the role of the Spirit in making prayer possible (Romans 8:26; Galatians 4:6).

Dibeela (2011) states that renewal and transformation will occur not only at a conceptual and structural level but also at a spiritual level when we learn again to pray as a body.

From the perspective of Eerdsman (2001), "Prayer is not a 'spare wheel' that you pull out when in trouble but a 'steering wheel' that directs the right path throughout one's life." Some Christians only pray whenever they are in difficulty or when a need in their life is to be met. This should not be so. Christians are admonished to pray without ceasing and not to faint.

CHAPTER 6

RESULTS OF PRAYER

I was diagnosed with uterine fibroids before having my second child, Phylicia. My General Practitioner feared that I would not have a normal pregnancy, and even if I did, she would have to be delivered via a C-section. My fear of going under the surgeon's knife drove my prayer life into overdrive. My prayers were answered when she was born via normal delivery, as was her sister, Carima, 17 months later.

It is many years later, and there are no signs or symptoms that warrant medical attention. Whenever the doctors give me a diagnosis, I go to the Specialist, the Great Physician, and it is His report that I continue to believe and prove to be true.

In His Word, God promises that healing belongs to us. There are many instances where Jesus, during His ministry, healed the sick. Sickness is not of God; it is a plan of the enemy, so His children should claim healing as our portion. The Word of God says in **Isaiah 53:4-5**, ***"Surely he hath borne our griefs, and carried our sorrows: yet we did esteem him*** *stricken, smitten of God, and afflicted. But he was wounded for our transgressions, he was bruised for our iniquities: the chastisement of our peace was upon him; and with his stripes we are healed."* With His stripes, we are healed. Jesus took all sickness and disease away from us when He was whipped and then crucified that fateful day on the cross, so now, as believers, we need to claim that promise.

The best way to claim that promise is through prayer. When we pray God's words back to Him, He will show up because He honours His word above His name. Believers need to use prayer to access the promises God made to us. We see in **James 5:16** clear instructions on how we should access healing. It states, *"Confess your faults one to another, and pray one for another, that ye may be healed. The effectual fervent prayer of a righteous man availeth much."* So, let us pray without ceasing to access our healing.

CHAPTER 7

TITHING

Ridolfi (2005) reports that from ancient times, the tenth part of a person's income and/or property devoted to religious use as an offering or to political use as tax or tribute has been known as tithe. Throughout ancient history, the tithe has been taught as an ideal of Christian giving. Old English law collected the tithe of crops and stored them in tithe barns. Although not practiced by the majority of Christians, the idea that one-tenth belongs to God is a living reality understood by churches but not practiced in all of them.

The word 'tithe' in the Old Testament is translated from the Hebrew word 'ma`ăśēr' and in the New Testament from the Greek word 'éna dékato'. In both instances, the meaning is the same. They refer to 'a tenth part'.

Dunlap (2009) points out that the word tithe is not taken from the religious world but from the world of mathematics or finance in both languages. Tithe first appears in Scripture (Genesis 14:20) when Abraham gave Melchizedek, the King of Salem, a tithe of the spoils from defeating the enemies of Sodom. Though this does not seem to be a specific command of God in this instance, Abraham gave his ten percent as an expression of unconstrained worship of God. This comes entirely from a place of gratitude and not obligation.

McGuckin (2004) states that tithing is referred to as an investment in God. **Malachi 3:10** admonish us to; ***"Bring ye all the tithes into the storehouse, that there may be meat in mine house, and prove me now herewith saith the Lord of hosts, if I will not open you the windows of heaven, and pour you out a blessing, that there shall not be room enough to receive it."***

Giving a tenth teaches us to put God first in our lives. He exhorts against robbing God. Our offerings do not begin until after we tithe. We should give more. God will rebuke Satan so he cannot steal our blessings. The local church is to be the recipient of our tithes.

Bernard (2010) points out that nowhere does the New Testament expressly command Christians to tithe. However, as believers, we are to be generous in sharing our material possessions with the poor and for the support of Christian ministry. Christ Himself is our model in giving. Giving is to be voluntary, willing, cheerful, and given in light of our accountability to God. Giving should be systematic and by no means limited to a tithe of our incomes. We recognize that all we have is from God. We are called to be faithful stewards of all our possessions (Romans 14:12; 1st Corinthians 9:3 – 14; 16: 1- 3; 2nd Corinthians 8:9).

Bernard describes tithing as the missing link in spiritual growth and maturity. He believes that in tithing, we thank God for our blessings and have faith that He will provide for us no matter the circumstances. The writer adds that the interesting thing about Renewal and Transformation is that we cannot choose some areas and ignore others. We must position ourselves to be renewed and transformed in all areas of our lives. Giving a tenth teaches us to put God first in our lives.

Tithing is an act of allegiance to God and also an act of thanksgiving. Like prayer and fasting, tithing is an act of worship as it ministers to the needs of others and has spiritual benefits for the giver.

I totally agree with Brown (2003) that applying the tithing principle can become a permanent gauge to assess the response of God's people to God's generous outpouring toward the objects of His love and affection. Hence, it is institutionalized as a way to shepherd the heart. Against this background, it is fair to say that the tithe belongs to God and consequently is holy or set apart for God's purpose (Leviticus 27:30).

The writer explains further that tithing is an act by which we concede that God is both our Sovereign Lord and the source of everything. Therefore, every time we return our tithes and offerings to God, we demonstrate our acceptance of our relationship with Him. It is proof of our acknowledgement of God as Creator and that we accept His ownership of who we are and what we have (Psalm 24:1).

Lawson (2010) challenges church members of the twenty-first century. He states that if we have been fasting, praying, and tithing and have yet to receive answers, we should carefully check our attitude. If our hearts are open and we have been giving – "not grudgingly or of necessity" - God will show us where we have erred. The writer points out that if we have been discouraged from fasting, praying, and tithing by lack of results in the past, God is giving us a chance to return to the Biblical fasting, prayer, and tithing – which the writer states constitute true worship – which always brings the desired result(s).

Having reviewed the literature on the biblical principles of fasting, prayer, and tithing and having experienced for myself the positive effects of these disciplines, I am convinced that if Christians practice these disciplines consistently and in the prescribed manner, they will indeed facilitate the growth and renewal in the worship experience of any church.

CHAPTER 8

BENEFITS OF TITHING

While in college, we survived on just my husband's salary. At the end of one month in particular, I was at my wit's end as to how all our bills would be paid. So, out of sheer desperation, I decided to pay my tithe and just let everything else fall into place. Before the week was out, I got a call from Bunny, my husband, telling me that his mom was visiting from England and wanted to meet up with the Family. During that meeting, each of us, including the three children, received an envelope with some British pounds. In addition to that, she took us to the supermarket on an open budget.

Just imagine how trusting God and following His principles of tithing can benefit us. That testimony shows that God can and will show up for us mightily once we put action behind our faith. We go back to **Malachi 3:11**, which says, ***"And I will rebuke the devourer for your sakes, and he shall not destroy the fruits of your ground; neither shall your vine cast her fruit before the time in the field, saith the Lord of hosts."*** This scripture means that when we bring our tithes into God's storehouse, He will not only pour out blessings that we do not have room to receive, but He will also protect what we have so that the enemy does not steal them.

Remember, the enemy comes to kill, steal, and destroy, but Christ came that we may have life and have it more abundantly, as stated in St. John 10:10. When we adhere to the principles of tithing, God will keep a special watch over all that He has entrusted to us. He will ensure that we have life and have it more abundantly, so provision will always come.

CHAPTER 9

CONCLUSION

In order to get its perspective right, the Church must reexamine its claim to be the 'Body of Christ' in the world. In a re-examination of this claim, members of the 'Body' will find fulfillment in the call to discipleship, which involves a life-changing decision that can only benefit our lives and the lives of those we touch.

According to Nembhard (2005), when an individual becomes a Christian, he/she acquires a new outlook and attitude towards things. This new outlook and attitude towards things will lead the believer to a desire to observe the Biblical principles, which lead to spiritual growth and renewal.

The Biblical principles Christians are expected to adhere to could be regarded as 'Disciplines' of the Christian faith. A discipline is defined as 'training or a pattern of behaviour that develops self-control or character.' I agree that Spiritual disciplines help us develop characteristics and patterns that eventually lead to growth in our spiritual lives and maturity.

The three Biblical principles observed in this publication are among these 'disciplines.' Fasting has often been referred to as a neglected discipline, even more so in the world of fast foods and the tendency to excesses. Fasting is a private matter between the believer and God, though there is a time for corporate or public fasting. Fasting, therefore, should not be seen as a means to an end but a way by which we diligently seek the presence of God. Therefore, the Church is commissioned to fast, as according to Dunlop et al., "More than any one single discipline, fasting reveals the things that control us."

I agree that fasting is not a Christian diet. One should not, therefore, fast to lose weight, although weight loss is a usual side effect. Except you put prayer with your fasting, there is no need to fast. Merely going without food is starving. When you fast, you should focus on prayer and God's Word. Part of the sacrifice of fasting, seeking God, and studying His word is that normal activity fades into the background. It is a constant means of renewing ourselves spiritually, and coupled with prayer, it is life-creating and life-changing.

Robert Foster stated, "Prayer is the central avenue that God uses to transform us." The word of God declares that children of God should pray without ceasing. Therefore, I concur that if we agree with this statement, the importance of the discipline and/or principle cannot be overemphasised.

Franklin (2006), a renowned theologian, asserts that God's favour is not for those with right beliefs but for those with right actions. The Church, therefore, has a responsibility to not only believe Biblical principles but to teach and practice them so that the life of the believer can be renewed and transformed.

As believers and members of the Body of Christ, each of us has been called to stewardship. Romans 12:1 declares that the faithful steward serves God in response to God's bountiful grace.

In addition to the observance of fasting and prayer, stewardship also includes giving of our financial resources to the work of the Church. According to the scriptures, this giving, which includes our tithes, should be regular, proportionate, and joyful.

Whenever the believer tithes, he/she recognizes that giving to God plays a significant part in his/her life. It shows concern about the church being able to meet the needs of the ministry and mission. Seeing then that we have been called into fellowship with the Lord, our actions should reflect Biblical principles that will lead to the growth of the Church.

One of the specific objectives of any church should be to respond to the spiritual, social, and economic needs of all congregants. I am therefore of the opinion that if, as a Church, we believe, teach, and practice the Biblical principles of fasting, prayer, and tithing as we ought, then the vision of renewal and transformation will become a reality. The Church would have fulfilled her mission of 'reaching the lost at any cost.'

CHAPTER 10

PERSONAL EVALUATION

In order to aid in the renewal and transformation of the worship experience in your local church, I invite you, my reader, to reflect on the following questions. It is my fervent hope and prayer that having honestly answered these questions, you will be able to assist in enlightening others in order to help in making a marked difference in the worship experience and growth of your Church.

Questions

1. How much do you know about fasting as a Biblical principle?
2. How often do you fast?
3. What benefits, if any, do you derive from fasting?
4. What other Biblical principles do you practice along with fasting?
5. How often do you pray?
6. How satisfied are you with your prayer life?
7. What type of prayer do you most often pray?

8. Are you always satisfied with the result/s of your prayers?
9. Does your church teach and practise tithing?
10. Do you practise tithing?
11. What percentage of your income/earnings is given for tithes?
12. How often do you tithe?
13. What is your greatest motivation for tithing?
14. What is the most challenging aspect of tithing for you?
15. Do you believe someone in debt or with pressing financial obligations should tithe?

BIBLIOGRAPHY

Bernard, H. Rt. Rev. (2010) *Tithing an Expression of Worship.* UCJCI

Eerdsman and Brill (2001). *The Encyclopedia of Christianity Volumes 2&4*

Hayford, J. W. (2002) *Prayer is Invading the Impossible.* Bridge – Logos

McGuckin, J. A. (2004). *The Westminister Handbook of Patristic Theology*

Nembhard, W. (2005). *Christian Stewardship Roots and Fruits.* Faith Works Press

Omartian, S. (2004). *The Prayer That Changes Everything.* Harvest House Publishers

Ridolfi, B. (2005). *The Ultimate Bible Answers Book*

Rodgers, B. (2006). *101 Reasons to Fast.* Charisma House

Smith, A. (1991). *Emerging From Innocence.* Eureka Press

Youngblood, R. F. (1995). *Nelson's New Illustrated Bible Dictionary*

ABOUT THE AUTHOR

Cherry Brown-Graham is a Retired Teacher, Trained Guidance Counselor, and a member of the Board of Elders at Salem United Church (United Church in Jamaica and the Cayman Islands. She is a mother of three adult children (two daughters and a son). Cherry is actively involved in Church and community activities and is passionate about the welfare of children.